SURVIVING CAPTIVITY WITH
THE U.S. AIR FORCE

ELITE FORCES SURVIVAL GUIDE SERIES

Elite Survival
Survive in the Desert with the French Foreign Legion
Survive in the Arctic with the Royal Marine Commandos
Survive in the Mountains with the U.S. Rangers and Army
  Mountain Division
Survive in the Jungle with the Special Forces "Green Berets"
Survive in the Wilderness with the Canadian and Australian
  Special Forces
Survive at Sea with the U.S. Navy SEALs
Training to Fight with the Parachute Regiment
The World's Best Soldiers

Elite Operations and Training
Escape and Evasion
Surviving Captivity with the U.S. Air Force
Hostage Rescue with the SAS
How to Pass Elite Forces Selection
Learning Mental Endurance with the U.S. Marines

Special Forces Survival Guidebooks
Survival Equipment
Navigation and Signaling
Surviving Natural Disasters
Using Ropes and Knots
Survival First Aid
Trapping, Fishing, and Plant Food
Urban Survival Techniques

SURVIVING CAPTIVITY WITH
THE U.S. AIR FORCE

CHRIS McNAB

Introduction by Colonel John T. Carney. Jr., USAF–Ret.
President, Special Operations Warrior Foundation

MASON CREST PUBLISHERS

This edition first published in 2003
by Mason Crest Publishers Inc.
370 Reed Road, Broomall, PA, 19008

Library of Congress Cataloging-in-Publication Data available

ISBN 1-59084-010-0

Editorial and design by
Amber Books Ltd.
Bradley's Close
74–77 White Lion Street
London N1 9PF

Project Editor Chris Stone
Designer Simon Thompson
Picture Research Lisa Wren

Printed and bound in Malaysia

10 9 8 7 6 5 4 3 2 1

ACKNOWLEDGMENT
For authenticating this book, the Publishers would like to thank the Public Affairs Offices of the U.S. Special Operations Command, MacDill AFB, FL.; Army Special Operations Command, Fort Bragg, N.C.; Navy Special Warfare Command, Coronado, CA.; and the Air Force Special Operations Command, Hurlbert Field, FL.

IMPORTANT NOTICE
The survival techniques and information described in this publication are for use in dire circumstances where the safety of the individual is at risk. Accordingly, the publisher cannot accept any responsibility for any prosecution or proceedings brought or instituted against any person or body as a result of the uses or misuses of the techniques and information within.

DEDICATION
This book is dedicated to those who perished in the terrorist attacks of September 11, 2001, and to the Special Forces soldiers who continually serve to defend freedom.

Picture Credits
Corbis: 11, 14, 22, 26, 28, 34, 36, 38, 42; TRH: 8, 10, 12, 13, 18, 20, 44, 47, 53, 54
Illustrations courtesy of De Agostini UK and the following supplied by Patrick Mulrey: 21, 24, 30, 31, 32, 33, 37, 41, 48, 55
Front cover: **TRH** (inset), **Corbis** (main)

CONTENTS

INTRODUCTION

Elite forces are the tip of Freedom's spear. These small, special units are universally the first to engage, whether on reconnaissance missions into denied territory for larger, conventional forces or in direct action, surgical operations, preemptive strikes, retaliatory action, and hostage rescues. They lead the way in today's war on terrorism, the war on drugs, the war on transnational unrest, and in humanitarian operations as well as nation building. When large scale warfare erupts, they offer theater commanders a wide variety of unique, unconventional options.

Most such units are regionally oriented, acclimated to the culture and conversant in the languages of the areas where they operate. Since they deploy to those areas regularly, often for combined training exercises with indigenous forces, these elite units also serve as peacetime "global scouts" and "diplomacy multipliers," a beacon of hope for the democratic aspirations of oppressed peoples all over the globe.

Elite forces are truly "quiet professionals": their actions speak louder than words. They are self-motivated, self-confident, versatile, seasoned, mature individuals who rely on teamwork more than daring-do. Unfortunately, theirs is dangerous work. Since "Desert One"—the 1980 attempt to rescue hostages from the U.S. embassy in Tehran, for instance—American special operations forces have suffered casualties in real world operations at close to fifteen times the rate of U.S. conventional forces. By the very nature of the challenges which face special operations forces, training for these elite units has proven even more hazardous.

Thus it's with special pride that I join you in saluting the brave men and women who volunteer to serve in and support these magnificent units and who face such difficult challenges ahead.

Colonel John T. Carney, Jr., USAF–Ret.
President, Special Operations Warrior Foundation

There are two types of parachute jump: High Altitude High Opening (HAHO) and High Altitude Low Opening (HALO).

THE USAF AND PRISONERS

Pilots in combat, and in particular the pilots of the United States Air Force, almost always operate over enemy lines. This means that if they are shot down and survive, there is a big risk that they will become prisoners of war.

Ever since pilots took to the skies on combat missions, they have run the risk of becoming prisoners of war, otherwise known as **POWs**. During World War II, huge numbers of U.S. and **Allied** fighters and bombers were shot down over Germany, occupied Europe, and in Asian countries during the war against Japan. They were lucky to survive, but danger still faced them. Some were killed by angry crowds of people as soon as they landed in their parachutes. Some were forced to go into hiding and attempt long and dangerous journeys to escape the enemy. Yet others were captured, and they ended up as POWs.

In prison, the prison officers tried to get as much information out of them as possible. This process is called "**interrogation.**" Sometimes, the interrogators tried to trick the pilot into releasing important and secret information about his battle plans. Other times, they actually tortured the man to get him to speak. The treatment depended very much on who was in charge in the prison and what sort of personalities the prison guards had.

This U.S. para is carrying the infamous Bazooka antitank rocket, which can fire a 60-mm rocket a distance of 1,948 feet (594 m).

In the history of the United States air forces, one of the worst places to become a prisoner was over North Vietnam during the **Vietnam War**. North Vietnam was a communist country attempting to take over South Vietnam. From 1965, U.S. aircraft started to bomb North Vietnam when it became involved in the war. On February 13, 1965, President Lyndon B. Johnson authorized Operation "**Rolling Thunder**"—one of the biggest bombing campaigns in history. Only nine months later, over a million tons of U.S. bombs had exploded inside North Vietnam— around 800 tons of bombs every single day. Rolling Thunder lasted for three years, and the **USAF**, U.S. Navy, and U.S. Marine Corps aircraft flew more than 304,000 missions.

Bombing raids over North Vietnam during the Vietnam War were conducted by B52 Stratofortress aircraft. Working in groups of three, B52s could bomb a target area of three square miles (4.8 sq km).

The SA-2 Guideline, which was the main surface-to-air missile of the North Vietnamese in the fight against America during the Vietnam War.

The U.S. had more airborne weaponry available to them than any nation on Earth. Aircraft such as the Phantom, Thunderchief, Skyhawk, and Skyraider flew right into the heart of enemy territory. There they dropped bombs and destroyed their targets, before attempting to fly back to the safety of South Vietnam. The power of this airborne armada was amazing. Yet North Vietnam did not intend to take this punishment lying down.

As Rolling Thunder intensified, the North Vietnamese started to build up more and more weaponry designed to shoot American aircraft down. In 1965, heavy **machine guns** were North Vietnam's main weapon. The danger of these to U.S. aircraft was very real. U.S. aircraft had to fly through storms of bullets, which took a heavy toll on aircraft and pilots—over 80 percent of the 3,000 American aircraft lost in the war were simply shot down by guns. By

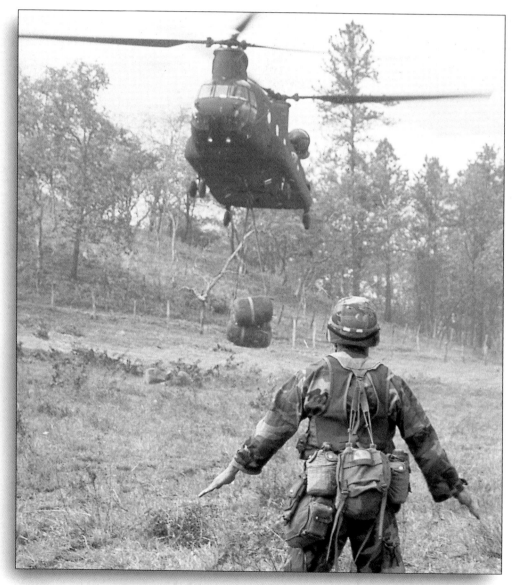

A pilot who is shot down will often activate a homing beacon. This emits a signal that gives a rescue helicopter a precise location.

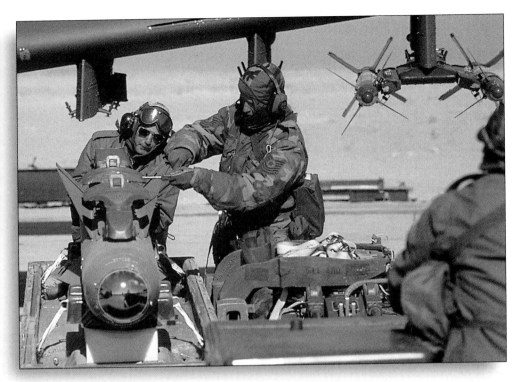

U.S. Air Force soldiers with an AGM-65 Maverick ground-to-air missile during the Gulf War in 1991. The airplane is an A-10 Thunderbolt.

1967 the situation was even worse. North Vietnam had acquired one of the most lethal air defense systems anywhere in the world. It had purchased from Russia a terrifying new missile called the **SA-2 Guideline**. The Guideline was a type of missile known as a surface-to-air missile (**SAM** for short). Once it was fired, it flew to its target using radar. It could hit American aircraft at around 69,060 feet (18,000 meters). This meant that U.S. pilots had to fly through bullets at low levels and dodge Guidelines at high levels. In addition to the lethal North Vietnamese air defenses, the U.S. pilots also faced the North Vietnamese Air Force (NVAF). In 1967, North Vietnam had an air force of around 80 fighters, mainly MiG jet fighters. MiGs were maneuverable and powerful aircraft, which in the Vietnam War usually had the advantage of operating over their own territory with SAMs to help them win.

Because of all the weapons North Vietnam had at its disposal, many U.S. aircraft were shot down. Some 586 USAF pilots were captured or declared missing between 1962 and 1973. In 1967 alone, 297 American aircraft were destroyed on Rolling Thunder missions. If the pilot survived, both American and North Vietnamese soldiers would rush to try to get the pilot before the other. Massive effort went into rescuing U.S. pilots who had received years of expensive aviation training and possessed valuable

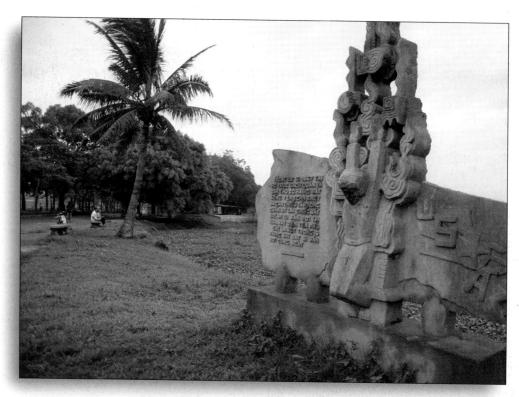

A monument to captured U.S. pilots in Hanoi, Vietnam. At the close of the Vietnam War, some 2,387 servicemen were also listed as missing.

information about U.S. aircraft. Yet sadly, the North Vietnamese often got there before the pilots' comrades, and they became prisoners of one of the cruelest regimes in history.

Captured American pilots were used by North Vietnam for **propaganda** and information. This actually saved them from being immediately killed. Instead, they were often paraded through the streets and filmed for North Vietnamese newsreels, then taken to one of a number of prisons in the city or district of Hanoi, the capital of North Vietnam. Among the worst of these was a prison called Hoa Lo Prison in the center of Hanoi, which the U.S. pilots nicknamed the "**Hanoi Hilton.**" Many other prisons also became infamous.

EJECTION SEATS

When pilots in a modern jet are shot down, the best way to escape is by using their ejection seats. These are the seats in which they fly the aircraft. If they need to escape from the aircraft, they can do so by pulling a lever that detonates a small explosive charge under the seat. At the same time, the cockpit glass flies off and the pilots are blown clear of the aircraft, still in their seats. This is a painful experience—pilots will travel several hundred feet (many tens of meters) in less than a second—but at least they are alive. Once they are clear of the aircraft, their parachutes open, and they float back down to earth.

In all these places, horrifying torture became a daily reality for the vast majority of captured airmen. The torture was inventive and cruel. It was often kept up for many days, even weeks. The aim was to break down the pilot's determination to withhold information so that he would tell military secrets to the North Vietnamese. The torture was so bad that many American pilots finally broke down and gave information. But this was usually only after many months, even years, of heroic resistance.

Because of the experience in Vietnam, all pilots in the USAF are now trained in the skills of surviving prison and interrogation, or evading capture in the first place. This program of training is known as **SERE**. SERE stands for Survival, Evasion, Resistance, Escape—the key elements a pilot needs if he or she is shot

A pilot of a P–51B Mustang in 1944. The rank insignia on his cap indicates he is a captain.

RESCUE IN VIETNAM

During the Vietnam War, rescuing pilots was often as dangerous a mission as the original bombing operation. On one rescue mission, U.S. helicopters and aircraft set out to rescue a navigator of a EB-66 aircraft that had been shot down just near the border of North Vietnam. The downed airman was on the run for 12 days, and in the time it took to rescue him, three helicopters were shot down by machine-gun fire and an OV-10 Bronco reconnaissance aircraft was shot down by an SA-2 Guideline missile. This resulted in 10 airmen dead, another one captured, besides the one who ended up on the run in the jungle. He was finally rescued after 10 days of dodging the enemy and living off the land.

down behind enemy lines. Survival means staying alive and living off the land for weeks at a time, even when the availability of food and water is low. Evasion means avoiding the enemy, and moving only when it is safe. Resistance is training in standing up to interrogation and not giving away vital information. Finally, Escape means just what it says—escaping from captivity and finding your way to safety.

In this book, we will look at how American pilots train to cope with the worst that captivity can throw at them. We will learn from the experts how to keep mind and body healthy, and how to stay focused on never giving in to the enemy.

BEING A PRISONER

Being captured by the enemy can be a terrifying experience. Your future seems entirely in the hands of your captors, and you do not know when you will see your loved ones again. Members of the U.S. Air Force are trained in the art of mental resilience so they can survive this harrowing experience.

One of the first things a U.S. pilot must do when training to survive captivity is find out what being a prisoner is really like. For an elite and highly trained pilot, courage and endurance are needed in major quantities if he or she is to survive a period in captivity. The enemy will understand how important their prisoner is. All their efforts will be to extract as much valuable information out of that person as possible.

Unfortunately, many governments around the world do not have a belief in human rights. This can mean that torture might be used to extract information if soldiers are unwilling to share their knowledge (and being elite soldiers, that is almost always the case). Thus a terrible battle begins—the captor using all the means at his disposal to forcibly pull information from captives' lips, and the captives relying on their training, but more importantly on their strength of will and intelligence, to resist giving away vital facts. It is an immense test of resolve.

While being interrogated, this soldier is made to kneel in a stressful position. After a few hours, this will become incredibly painful.

Pilots who eject from their aircraft always carry a basic survival pack. This contains equipment such as waterproof matches, a small fishing kit, a survival blanket, a survival knife, and a compass.

Whatever the mental strength of the prisoners, the odds are stacked against them if they are in the hands of an intelligent interrogator. Many countries spend as much time and money investigating how to make people talk as others do in resisting interrogation. Furthermore, expert interrogators will usually know exactly what type of training the soldier has had for this situation. That means they know exactly how the person will resist.

But this is not the full picture. When we tend to think of the horrors of detention, we often focus on the experience of torture. Yet this is only one possible element of detention. It is also far from the most common. From the point of view of survival, everything about being a POW is usually designed to make the prisoner feel depressed, and leave the captive bored, lonely, uncomfortable, and confused.

A prisoner must calm his mind if he is to cope with the terrible boredom of captivity.

Once he or she in this condition, it is easier for the captors to break the captive's will and make the captive talk.

One of the biggest problems facing a captured pilot is loneliness and boredom. Pilots tend to be people who live exciting lives with lots of friends around them and plenty of activity. Captors often realize this, so they tend to place elite soldiers in places where they are isolated from people. The only people they see usually are the prison guards. The prison cell in which they are held is frequently very small. This means that the soldiers cannot move around as much as they would like. These conditions can start to break the pilots' will if they are not strong people and well trained. First, they may become less interested in looking after themselves. The outside world can start to seem less real. These feelings are what the captors want, because they enable them to draw out information from the

He can also relieve boredom by moving around.

prisoners. The reason for this is that the information does not feel as important to the pilots as it did when they were on the outside.

Another problem for pilot survivors is that if they are held long enough, they can begin to feel safe in the prison. This happens because they forget what it is like to live outside. This may seem strange, but remember that in the Vietnam War some pilots were kept on their own for two or three years without any contact with their friends or relatives. They did not even know what was happening in the news. The prison became their entire world.

In these situations, the only human contact the prisoners receive is that of the guards. This can actually mean that the prisoners look forward to the guards' visits—anything to break the hideous boredom. The guards will often pretend to be the prisoners' friends

In 1973, the North Vietnamese released 512 American prisoners of war (some of which are shown here) in "Operation Homecoming."

so they will trust them and start to talk. Trained pilots will recognize that this is what the captors are trying to do, however, and they will always watch what they say. Yet, the longer prisoners spend in detention, the further removed they may feel from their families and friends, and the more depressed they can become. Thus, they will probably come to welcome any human contact, and the enemy interrogators may cleverly fill this gap with their own people.

Of course, not all prisoners are kept alone. Some are kept in cells with one or two other people, while others are packed tightly into small rooms with lots of prisoners. This last situation can be as depressing as being by yourself. With little space, it is difficult to move around, the cell gets incredibly hot, and people can start to argue with

BURMA–THAILAND RAILWAY

During World War II, the Japanese army was famous for being cruel to its prisoners. A grim example from history is the Burma–Thailand railroad network, which was built by Allied POWs and native laborers. Prisoners were given almost no food and water, even though they had to work over 14 hours each day. They had to lay railroad lines in the blistering heat, while mosquitoes gave them malaria, an illness that can be life-threatening. The railroad was thousands of miles long, and many prisoners could not survive the tough regime. The type of work forced upon the prisoners resulted in the deaths of some 102,000 prisoners.

each other because of the frustration. Again, this is something that the captors may be doing deliberately. If the people in the prison cell fall out with one another, they will not be as loyal to their comrades, and they might be more likely to talk.

Another problem associated with being held captive is that time goes incredibly slowly. Often the prisoner will not have anything to do at all—no books, no games, no possessions, nothing. This will cause time to pass incredibly slowly. Boredom will cause physical discomfort as the mind makes the body fidget in an attempt to find anything to do. This, in turn, leads to a build-up of anxiety, which over several months or years can crush the will to continue. It will even make you feel incredibly tired. Try sitting very still for a few hours without movement or entertainment.

Subjecting a prisoner to extremely loud music for many hours was a form of torture used during the Korean War (1950–53).

Your mind will start to feel very tired in spite of the fact that you are not physically working.

Not all prisoners are kept inside cells all day. Many POWs are made to work incredibly hard. This results in prisoners suffering from **fatigue**. Prisoners of war are often put to work as slave workers. Many prisons do work the prisoners hard. The hard work is made worse by a lack of proper food and rest. This can make the prisoners very weak and depressed. All prisoners should try to save as much energy as possible. That means resting when they are not working and trying to eat and drink as much as possible.

The combination of boredom, stress, overwork, and poor food mean that prisons are very unhealthy places. Military prison camps tend to make prisoners weak and undernourished. In this condition, the prisoner will be prone to get ill. A poor diet results in a poor **immune system**—the parts of the body that fights off illnesses. The prisoners are much more likely to contract illnesses, and the illnesses tend to be more serious when they do. Illness is not only a physical problem. It also makes POWs very unhappy and pessimistic, and they can start to worry much more about making it out of prison.

These factors are just a few of the things that assault the mind and body of a pilot under the detention of the enemy. Such conditions are faced by almost all those captured by an enemy. But for elite soldiers, there is the added problem that they will attract interrogation. Elite soldiers are more likely than, say, an army cook, to attract the attention of the special interrogator. The interrogator's purpose is to use physical or psychological methods to make the captive talk. As we shall see in the next chapter, their "skills" and tools can be very powerful.

INTERROGATION

You have to be tough to survive interrogation. The secret is not to keep reminding yourself of what you must not say, but not doing anything that might make your interrogation worse. It is a difficult balance, but one that elite soldiers are trained to master.

One of the first methods used by the interrogator is the actual room in which the prisoner is kept. American pilots in Vietnam's infamous Hanoi Hilton found themselves in squalid and tiny cells. These were often almost pitch black. They generally had no toilet facilities and were full of rats, cockroaches, and huge spiders. The prisoner thus became dirty and had to constantly fight off the often aggressive insects and animals.

The cell is important to the interrogator as a place from which the prisoner will long to escape. The interrogator will make the prisoner aware that all he or she has to do is talk, and then they will be given a clean cell, a hot bath, and proper food. Over time, the interrogator hopes that the prisoner will give up vital information just for physical comfort.

The interrogator, however, may choose a different environment for the prisoner. Sometimes he will deliberately make a room that contains absolutely nothing to do at all and nothing interesting to see. This is usually a featureless cell without natural light (thus the

A Korean soldier interrogates a Vietcong guerrilla. 47,000 Korean soldiers fought against the communists during the Vietnam War.

The "Hanoi Hilton," the horrifying destination for many U.S. airmen in Vietnam. Some walls of the prison had glass embedded in the top so that they were almost impossible to climb over without injury.

prisoner loses track of time and date), without noise, and with nothing to entertain. Clothing is also selected to be very soft so as to create little sensation on the skin. Research has shown that this form of torture—called "**sensory deprivation**"—is actually one of the cruelest things of all. Prisoners in these conditions become very worried and crave human contact very badly.

Both the filthy cell and the sensory-deprivation cell help the interrogator to show that he has absolute power over the prisoner's life. He can then start to ask the prisoner direct questions. Sometimes he might use physical punishment—torture—to try to get the person to speak. Yet there is another method of interrogation that does not involve violence. This is called "**brainwashing**."

During brainwashing, the prisoner will meet a smart interrogator. The interrogator then teaches the soldier why it is wrong that the prisoner's country is fighting against the enemy's country. This may seem harmless, but the interrogator will keep the "lessons" going for weeks at a time. The soldier will be kept awake at nights while these lessons are going on so that he becomes less able to resist what the interrogator is saying. The interrogator hopes that eventually the soldier will give in and admit that his country is wrong. Once he has done this, the interrogator can get information out of the soldier. He can also use him for propaganda purposes, putting him in films and magazines criticizing his own country.

If brainwashing does not work, physical torture might be used. Torture comes in many different types, and it would not be pleasant to list them all here. However, what the torturer is trying to do is to break the soldier's will through physical pain. If the soldier does not talk, the pain is increased. If he does talk, the pain is lessened. It has to be said that most people will eventually break under physical torture over a long period. However, in Vietnam and other conflicts, some American pilots held out for many months. One or two never gave up any valuable information, despite years of abuse at the hands of their captors.

Sometimes, interrogators will use more subtle methods of getting information out of the prisoner. One of the most cunning of these is the use of a person who pretends to be a prisoner, but who is actually working for the enemy. This person will get into discussions

Sometimes interrogation involves two interrogators. By both shouting at the prisoner at once, they can frighten and confuse the prisoner.

Putting a soaking wet towel over the prisoner's head until he could not breathe was a common form of torture used in the Vietnam War.

with the other prisoners. Because the other prisoners think that the person is one of them, they might tell him some of the secrets they are holding. The "**double agent**" will be very hard to spot since they are specially trained to deceive the other prisoners.

There are no hard and fast rules for surviving an interrogation. However, USAF pilots and elite soldiers worldwide have rules about what to do and what not to do:

- Do not challenge your interrogators—this will only make them angry and may make them hurt you more during the interrogation.
- Focus on things that make you calm. For example, if you are being shouted at in a room with a window, focus your attention more on the warm sunlight outside than on the stream of abuse.
- During brainwashing, pretend that you are interested in what they are saying. This will make the enemy think they are making progress, and you will have time to save your physical energy. But be careful; the interrogators will be experts in spotting whether you are lying or not. Do not make things too easy for them.

- Keep reminding yourself there are people outside the prison who are working to get you released or win the war and free you. This will give you hope that the interrogation is not going to last forever.
- If you have to give information, hold on for a few days. Your comrades back at base will know that you have been captured, and they can change their plans in case you give anything away.
- If you are going into action in a group, make up a false story about your mission. If your group is captured, you can all come out with the same false story and possibly convince your enemy that you do not know anything important.

These steps can help a soldier survive interrogation, but it will still be tough. The most important thing is that the soldier still believes

Nonviolent interrogation is often used as a way of befriending the prisoner in the hope that he offers to talk voluntarily.

that he or she can hold out. The soldier who has the attitude "You cannot beat me," is most likely to survive mentally. So what do you need to do to survive the rest of prison life? This is the subject of the next chapter.

READING LIES

A trained interrogator can often tell when someone is lying because of the things they do with their body and words. These include:

- Rubbing their nose or ear nervously while talking.
- The person keeps looking up while talking—this often means that the person is using their imagination to invent a story.
- The person's feet and hands are always shifting and twisting.
- The story does not come out easily. When people are telling the truth, they usually speak quickly and confidently.
- The person cannot look the interrogator in the eye, though this could be caused by fear.

SURVIVING PRISON LIFE

Prison life varies tremendously from place to place. Sometimes prisoners are treated well, sometimes very badly. The USAF pilot is trained to survive whatever the circumstances.

All elite soldiers go through SERE training. This is to help them survive capture by the enemy. SERE training is designed to be as realistic as possible. The instructors will dress up as enemy guards and speak in foreign languages. The "prisoners" will be shouted at, kept awake throughout the nights, and questioned all the time to try to get information.

This type of training can be very hard, but it is important. By being trained in this way, a soldier will know something of what might happen if he or she is captured. This means that the experience will not be as much of a shock, and the soldier can think clearly about how to survive.

However, training can only teach so much about surviving captivity. The most important thing is the soldiers' characters. If people give in whenever there are problems, or moan about their worries, then they are not likely to cope well with the experience of being held in captivity. Yet if they are disciplined, with a good sense of humor and a strong desire to come through alive, they have a much better chance of surviving until they are released.

A POW training center in Reno, Nevada. Barbed wire and razor wire fences are difficult to escape across, especially if they are electrified.

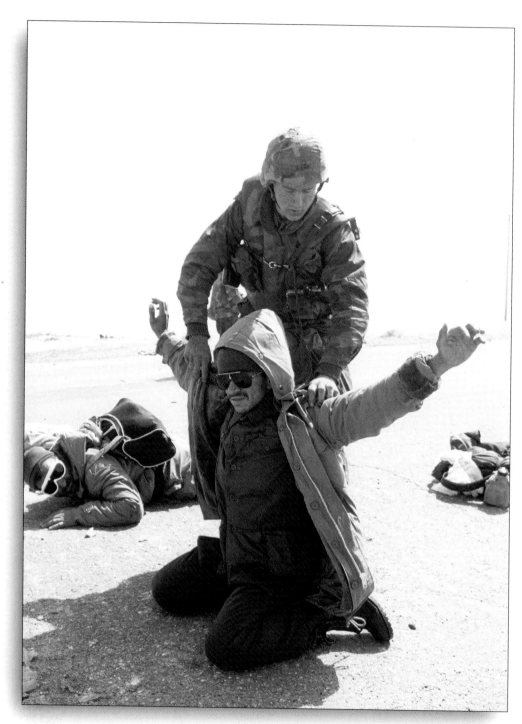

In the Gulf War, U.S. troops captured their first Iraqi prisoners on January 19, 1991. They went on to capture thousands.

Though character cannot be taught, there are some principles of survival that can be learned. The most important are listed here.

Control what can be controlled

In prison, the temptation is to feel that you are completely helpless and at the mercy of the prison guards. You must overcome this feeling if you are to survive for long periods. The first thing to do is to set up as much of a routine as possible. This helps you keep track of the days and feel like you are still in control of your life. There are many things prisoners can do with their time. Perhaps they can hold discussion groups with fellow prisoners at certain times. Or they

Prison guards throw rubbish deliberately into the prisoner's cell because a dirty cell makes life even more unpleasant for him.

could simply clean the corner of the cell. By doing simple things such as these, the soldiers will feel better about themselves and more in control. By feeling more in control, they are more likely to stay positive and believe that they will be rescued or escape.

Keep fit

Keeping fit in detention is not always easy, especially if you are held in cramped conditions and the food is poor. Fitness helps the mind to stay stronger, so the prisoner should try to keep up some form of exercise program. Work especially on the legs and arms, as you will need both to be strong if you are suddenly faced with the opportunity for a rescue attempt. If you are in very cramped

A U.S. pilot tends a garden in a Vietnamese prison. Such images were used by the North Vietnamese to suggest that they treated their prisoners well, but in reality they were regularly tortured.

conditions, simple stretching exercises and basic arm and leg strengthening exercises will stop muscles from wasting and help the mind stay healthier. However, there is one important point to remember: Prisoners should not exercise if they are very weak or ill. This is because it will burn up their energy, and they need all their energy to stay alive.

Keep the mind alert

Mental alertness is extremely difficult to maintain when you are isolated and bored. Try to develop mental projects for yourself—such as writing a book in your head (doing, say, a chapter each day). Basically, do anything to keep the brain active and sharp.

During the Vietnam War, some USAF prisoners set themselves amazing mental tasks to help them survive. One pilot built his dream home in his head. He did not just plan how his home would be built, but actually imagined it being built in the same time as it would take in reality. Working from the foundations to the roof, he "built" the home in just over a year. It was a long and exhausting project, but the important point was that it helped time to pass. If you are a prisoner, doing such mental tasks will also make you feel that your own personality and intelligence is not lost in the experience of captivity.

Do not make your enemy hate you

However much they dislike their captors, captured soldiers should never go out of their way to insult or challenge the enemy. The enemy does, after all, have control over how much food and water the prisoners receive, and what sort of treatment they get. If prisoners do something to make the captors unhappy, the prisoners' situation could get much worse. As a prisoner, your priority should be survival, not winning your own private war. That is why you should be as cunning as possible with your captors. Strike up conversations with ones who are in any way friendly. This will make them less willing to harm you, and it may even bring about better treatment. Also, it may make them give away information about the way that the prison works. This could help you escape.

Help each other

If pilots are in the company of other military prisoners, they should still respect the rank of other soldiers (though they should beware of giving away the rank of important officers to the captors). Being a prisoner should not be treated as a "time out" in military service. Instead, the soldiers should treat it as part of their operation and keep military discipline at all times. This also involves helping out their fellow prisoners. Being supportive of each other will make prison less lonely. A good group of comrades can help out when things get tough, and can also keep up a sense of humor, which can really help you survive mentally.

Plan to escape

Even if escape is almost impossible, it is still a good idea to plan such an attempt. This is not only because you may win your freedom. It also helps keep the mind alert and lively. Plan your escape as thoroughly as possible (see the next chapter) and keep on the

During SAS escape training, the soldier must escape from soldiers, tracker dogs, and helicopters for a period of about 24 hours.

A Vietcong suspect is tied up and blindfolded during U.S. operations by the 25th Infantry Division in Vietnam.

lookout for any moments when it can be put into action. By having an escape plan in the back of your mind, you will also feel more in control of your destiny and less helpless before the prison guards.

Following these principles and mental activities can make a period in detention survivable. A lot of these activities require good self-discipline to pursue. Again, this depends on your character. The main point is not to become dependent upon the prison environment, and to keep enough dignity to assure yourself that it is not where you belong.

SAS TRAINING

The British SAS has one of the toughest training courses in the world for surviving prison and interrogation. At the end of SAS training—the final stage of which takes place in the jungles of Borneo—there is an Escape and Evasion exercise. If soldiers are caught, they are "interrogated" by their instructors for several days. It is vital that the soldiers do not give away any important information during the interrogation. If they do, they will not be allowed to join the SAS. Often the soldiers are kept blindfolded for several days, left in cold cells for hours, shouted at, and even left in the middle of fields while cars drive at speed around them. All this happens when they are exhausted anyway from a punishing march across the mountains, and only the toughest soldiers keep their mouths shut.

ESCAPE

Escape is the most exciting thought for a prisoner. But an escape must be rigorously planned and executed if it is to succeed, which can be difficult if the prisoner is tired and hungry. Being recaptured is a very unpleasant prospect, because the prisoners' treatment at the hands of their captors is likely to be far worse than before they escaped.

There are no hard and fast rules about escaping from imprisonment. A successful escape plan depends on luck as much as planning. It has to be said that escape can be incredibly difficult from a maximum security military prison. Yet not all military prisons have high security. Because POWs are often captured in large numbers, many prisons are hastily built camps. The security on these may be open to an escape attempt. However, military prisons have lots of guards who are all heavily armed. Any attempt to escape will often result in death if you are seen. That is why you need a good escape plan.

When planning to escape, your mind should keep focused on the following points: Watch out for any routines in the prison that you can use to your advantage—times when there are fewer guards on duty, or times when vehicles make deliveries. Remember these patterns, and build up in your mind a profile of how the prison

Barbed or razor wire is usually found at the perimeter of prison camps. Since it snags on clothing, it is very difficult to climb over.

Watchtowers usually feature one or two soldiers armed with rifles and controlling spotlights.

operates. This should tell you when and where the security in the prison is at its weakest. This also involves using your senses. Keep eyes and ears open at all times to gather more and more information. Try to get friendly guards to reveal crucial information inadvertently. Also, try to get jobs within the prison that might put you in places from where it is easier to escape.

You must also have a plan. Escape can and does happen on the spur of the moment, but even if the occasion does occur, you should have planned in detail what your course of action will be. Planning helps the mind to stay in focus and helps you get ready for the escape event. Rehearse the escape in you mind time and time again, introducing various disasters to test whether your plan works or not. This basic mental preparation can help give you confidence during an actual escape attempt.

When the moment for escape comes, you must throw all your efforts into it. Your intention should be to get as far away from the prison as possible, to avoid being recaptured, and to get to safety. These are the skills of evasion.

Soldiers evading capture must cover as much ground as possible when it is safe to do so. During times of danger, they must lie low.

Evasion is a skill taught to most troops. It applies not only to those who have escaped, but also to those who have yet to be caught. Surviving in the wild while trying to evade capture is an extremely difficult situation. The body will quickly become tired and dirty. This may lead to depression, and the escaped prisoner can then lose the will to continue. Fear may also prey on the

Soldiers must not leave signs of their presence when evading capture. This soldier is taking food from a field while lying on his belly so that he does not leave footprints in the mud at the edge of the field.

mind, the fear of what will happen to you if you are captured or recaptured.

The way around these problems is to have a clear plan. The most essential points of evasion planning are:

- Have a clear idea of where you are going. Uncertainty can lead to despair, so soldiers must have some idea of what their objectives are. These should be broken down into hourly, daily, and weekly objectives so that time is tightly controlled.

- During the early stages of evasion, soldiers should try to put as much distance between themselves and the prison as possible. If only five miles (8 km) are traveled from the starting point, then that will give a possible 78 square mile area (125 sq km) for the

Camouflaged uniforms were first introduced in the French-Indian War of 1754–63, when a company of Rangers wore green and brown uniforms to help them ambush the French soldiers.

searchers to cover. The greater the distance from the prison, the more options the soldiers will have if they need to change their plan. Also, every mile walked can breed confidence in the soldiers and make them more certain that they are going to succeed.

- If you are evading capture, you should use your intelligence and training to avoid the pursuers. If you are moving through a civilian area, try to look as natural as possible; carrying a spade or similar civilian item can help you to blend in with others. Obviously, however, this depends on your having the ability to speak the language of the people around you. Do not try to communicate with them unless you have a perfect grasp of the language. Try to

TRACKING SKILLS

Tracking skills can be very useful for escaping soldiers. They help them to know where the enemy is and whether they are about to walk into a trap. Signs that the enemy is in the area are:

- Moved stones, crumbled stones, or those pressed into the earth.
- Bushes or grasses bent down—these show that an enemy patrol has passed by the area.
- Stains—blood, water, and crushed leaves.
- Dropped litter.
- Footprints pressed into mud or soil.

stay away from dogs. They are often the first to pick up on strangers.

- If you are in the countryside, you should occasionally walk in twisted, zigzagging patterns to throw off **tracker dogs** that are on your tail. If you do things like climb up and down trees, move across walls several times, and go in and out of streams, the tracker dogs will become confused and turn back on themselves.

- Make sure you get plenty to eat and drink on the journey and also that you let yourself sleep. Lack of food, drink, and sleep will make your mind confused. This, in turn, can lead to your making mistakes, which can then result in your being captured again. So sleep when necessary for short periods—even 20 minutes will help you to wake up with more energy and a clearer head. Steal food if possible to maintain your energy, but be aware not to leave any tracks or be detected. When stealing crops, a good method is to lie over the edge of the field so you do not leave footprints in the soil.

- Make sure that you never drop any litter. The enemy can use this material to track you.

By looking after the body as much as possible and by having a plan, the chances are that this, combined with a lot of luck, will mean that an escape attempt succeeds. Of course, this assumes that soldiers have a generally firm will. Regardless of training, soldiers attempting to escape must apply themselves with strength and learn to tolerate discomfort, pain, and fear along the way. Thankfully for elite USAF pilots, their initial training period should have provided these skills anyway.

SURVIVE IN THE WILDERNESS

Evasion is only one part of a successful escape attempt. Once soldiers escape, they must face the prospect of surviving in often hostile conditions with only the materials they have brought with them. Sometimes that may be nothing. Elite soldiers must learn to improvise if they are to survive.

The final element of this book is that of survival. Being in a wilderness without food, shelter, or water probably presents a bigger danger to life and health than the pursuers. The actual techniques of survival are not our focus here. Rather, what should be understood is how the environment affects the way your mind works and the will to survive.

We have already looked at the need for rest, food, and water. Shelter is just as important as these three. This applies even in warm countries, because the two biggest enemies of anyone exposed are cold and heat. Enduring extreme cold and extreme heat can lead to illnesses known as **hypothermia** and **hyperthermia**. Hypothermia (also called **exposure**) happens in situations of extreme cold. It is caused when the temperature in the middle of the human body falls below its safe level of 97.8–100.4°F (36–38°C). Hyperthermia (also called **heatstroke**)

A soldier dries out his feet while surviving in woodland. Leaving feet wet can literally make them rot, a condition called "trench foot."

Endurance is vital to survival, so training is hard. When a soldier is constantly running and moving, he can burn up 4,000 calories a day.

is the opposite—in very hot climates, the human body gets too warm, and the blood gets too thick to be pumped easily around the body by the heart.

Both of these illnesses can kill if they are not treated immediately. A person with hypothermia needs to be warmed up, whereas a person with hyperthermia needs to be cooled down. Even the early stages of these illnesses are a problem for the escaping prisoner, because they affect the ability to think and make clear decisions. A person with either problem will become disorientated, confused, depressed, and may even start to hallucinate. For escaping prisoners, this means they are likely to make mistakes that could lead them to be captured again.

To protect themselves from cold weather, soldiers must follow several rules:

- Keep the head and hands covered up at all times.
- Find a shelter, particularly at night. Old farm buildings can be good because they may have lots of hay and straw to make a warm bed. But make sure that you are not discovered there by a farmer or farm dog.
- Make sure you do not even begin an escape attempt if you do not have some form of appropriate clothing. There is no point in escaping only to die of exposure.
- Try to stay as dry as possible.
- Keep out of very cold winds which can take all the body warmth.

Extreme heat can be just as serious as extreme cold. The soldier will become tired and apathetic, and must follow commonsense precautions like staying out of the sun, and drinking as much as possible. Shelter is vital, especially in the desert regions (one **SAS** soldier walked 160 miles (255 km) through desert during the Gulf War while fleeing Iraqi soldiers). Find caves to shelter in or make shelters out of pieces of material. If you have some water, do not drink it all at once. Ration it out slowly. Do not eat if there is not much water.

A simple A-frame shelter can be made by using long boughs (branches) for the structure and large leaves to cover it.

When evading the enemy, soldiers must avoid unnecessary exposure to the elements and dehydration, all of which increase tiredness.

From a mental point of view, both heat and cold present the survival problem of fear. The escaping soldier will start to think about "freezing to death" or "dying of thirst." Believe it or not, just thinking about dying can make it more likely. Studies into people who have survived extreme survival situations usually showed that they never let go of the belief that they would survive. A strong mind seems to make the body stronger. Elite pilots and soldiers tend to have strong minds already from the hard training they have experienced. This gives them a good advantage when surviving an escape attempt.

In any survival situation, whether it is in a prison camp or on the run, having clear goals and a strong desire to survive are possibly the most important tools the soldier has in order to come out of the situation alive. Training does impart essential skills of survival, but the lesson seems to be that character can decide whether someone lives or dies in a survival or prison situation.

SKIN HEATING TECHNIQUE

The efficiency of this is best tested on your hands. If they are particularly cold, first touch them against a warm part of your body to remember their original temperature; then practice the following technique:

1) First imagine that hot blood is pumping right through the hands and into the fingertips.

2) While doing this, also imagine that you are immersing your hands in a thick, very warm, orange liquid.

3) As you do this, actually look at your hands and believe that you have total control over their temperature.

GLOSSARY

Allied When referring to World War II, "Allies" meant the countries that
fought against Germany and Japan.

Brainwashing Planting ideas and beliefs in someone's mind.

Double agent A secret agent who pretends to be working for one side but
is actually working for the enemy.

Exposure An illness that results from being exposed to the weather and
outdoors environment.

Fatigue A feeling of extreme tiredness that often makes a person confused
and depressed.

Hanoi Hilton The nickname American pilots gave to the Hoa Lo Prison
in North Vietnam during the Vietnam War.

Heatstroke A serious medical problem caused by a person
becoming too hot from exposure to the sun.

Hyperthermia Another name for heatstroke.

Hypothermia A serious medical problem caused by a person becoming
too cold.

Immune system In the human body, the immune system tries to fights off
illnesses and any germs that invade the body.

Interrogation Trying to get a prisoner to give important information by
force.

Machine guns Guns that fire bullets at a very fast rate.

POW An abbreviation of the words "Prisoner of War."

Propaganda Making many people believe in a particular view of events.

Rolling Thunder One of the largest bombing campaigns in history, when
the U.S. bombed North Vietnam between 1965 and 1968.

SA-2 Guideline A surface-to-air missile that the North Vietnamese used
to try to shoot down U.S. aircraft during the Vietnam War.

SAM A word that stands for surface-to-air missile. These missiles are
fired from the ground at targets in the air.

SAS The British Special Air Service—possibly the world's best elite unit.

Sensory deprivation When there is no noise, no light, nothing to entertain a prisoner, and no human company.

SERE An acronym that stands for Survival, Evasion, Resistance, Escape.

Tracker dogs A dog specially trained to track down people on the run.

USAF Stands for United States Air Force.

Vietnam War A war between North Vietnam and South Vietnam in which the U.S. fought between 1965 and 1972.

EQUIPMENT REQUIREMENTS

Compass
Flint and steel firelighter
Windproof matches
Striker board (for the matches)
Candle (some versions are edible
Magnifying glass
Flexible saw
Lock knife/Swiss Army knife
Sewing thread
Needles
Single-edged razor
Heliograph (a mirror for signaling)
Fishing gear

Wire snare
Whistle
Water bag
Water purification tablets
Bag closures
Wound closures
Antiseptic
Adhesive bandages
Sunblock/insect repellent
Safety pin
Pencil
Notepad
Signal flares

CHRONOLOGY

August 1, 1907   Aeronautical Division of the Signal Corps of the U.S. Army created.

July 18, 1914   Founding of the Aviation Section of the Signal Corps

1917   The United States enters World War I. It has one air force unit, the 1st Aero Squadron.

1918   World War I ends. The air units are now under the command of the U.S. Army and are called the U.S. Army Air Service. It now has a total of 740 aircraft.

1926   The U.S. Army Air Service is renamed the Army Air Corps.

1942   With the U.S. now in World War II, the Army Air Service becomes the United States Army Air Forces (USAAF).

1942–1945   U.S. aircraft fight throughout the war, and bring the war to a close with the dropping of the atomic bombs on Hiroshima and Nagasaki in Japan.

July 26, 1947   The U.S. Air Force is born as a military unit separate from the army.

1950–1953   USAF aircraft go into action against the North Koreans and Chinese in the Korean War.

1965–1975   The USAF goes to war in a ten-year conflict in Vietnam. It conducts some of the biggest operations in its history, including the massive bombing of North Vietnam in Operation Rolling Thunder (1965–1968).

1983	USAF aircraft support troops in seizing the Caribbean island of Grenada in Operation Urgent Fury.
1986	USAF bombers attack Libya in Operation El Dorado Canyon.
1990–1991	The Gulf War. In one of the biggest air wars since Vietnam, the USAF pounds Iraqi military targets.
1995	As part of NATO, American aircraft bomb targets in Serbia in an attempt to stop war atrocities that are being committed in the former Yugoslavia.
1999	U.S. jets go into action in Kosovo, former Yugoslavia. They attack Serbian military targets after Serbian troops expel millions of people from Kosovo.
2000	Operation Bolton. Guarding air bases in Iraq as part of enforcing the peace following the Gulf War in 1991.
2001	U.S. Air Force troops continue to be stationed in Bosnia and Kosovo, keeping the peace.
September 11, 2001	In response to terrorist attacks in America, the U.S. military, including U.S. Air Force troops, are put on the highest military alert since the Cuban Missile Crisis.

RECRUITMENT INFORMATION

There are over 200 careers in the U.S. Air Force, and each of them requires different qualifications and training. The USAF gives this advice to those who are still in school:

• Study hard. The USAF requires intelligent people who show that they can work hard, so do as best as you can at your schoolwork.
• Finish your education. The USAF does not take dropouts—show that you are strong enough to keep going.
• Do as many technical subjects as you can. Almost every Air Force career involves math and science, so try to do well in these subjects.
• Get to know your counselor. Find someone who can keep you on the right track for success.

To be considered for a career in the U.S. Air Force, candidates must be high school graduates, between 18–33 years of age, U.S. citizens, be physically fit, and have a four-year degree from an accredited college or university. There are no physical tests that need to be passed.

Once the soldier has passed initial selection, there follows six weeks of Basic Training at Lackland Air Force Base in Texas where the soldier is taught Air Force customs, how to drill, how to shoot a rifle, and the benefits of teamwork.

If you want to find out more about a career in the USAF, go to the website: www.airforce.com
It will give you all the information you need about USAF jobs, and directions to your nearest recruiting office.
Other useful websites include:
http://www.USAF2000.com
http://www.spacecom.af.mil
http://www.airforcehistory.com
http://www.af.mil
http://www.pdas.com

FURTHER READING

Bowman, Martin. *The USAF at War: From Pearl Harbor to the Present Day.* Somerset, England: Haynes Publications, 1995.

Bowman, Martin. *The USAF, 1947–99.* Gloucester, England: Sutton Publishing, 2000.

Boyne, Walter. *Beyond the Wild Blue: A History of the United States Air Force, 1947–1997.* New York: St. Martin's Press, 1997.

Dear, Ian. *Escape and Evasion: POW breakouts in World War II.* London: Cassell Academic, 2001.

Dick, Ron and Dan Patterson. *American Eagles: A History of the United States Air Force, Featuring the Collection of the US Air Force Museum.* Charlottesville, Va.: Howell Press, 1997.

Flach, Andrew. *The Official United States Elite Workout.* New York: Hatherleigh Press, 1999.

Hutton, Donald B. *Guide to Military Careers: Air Force, Army, Coast Guard, Marines, Navy.* New York: Barrons Educational Series, 1998.

Rochester, Stuart. *Honor Bound: American Prisoners of War in Southeast Asia 1961–1973.* Anapolis, Md.: United States Naval Institute, 1999.

Thompson, Wayne. *To Hanoi and Back: The US Air Force and North Vietnam 1966–73.* Washington, D.C.: Smithsonian Institution Press, 2000.

ABOUT THE AUTHOR

Dr. Chris McNab has written and edited numerous books on military history and elite forces survival. His publications to date include *German Paratroopers of World War II, The Illustrated History of the Vietnam War, First Aid Survival Manual,* and *Special Forces Endurance Techniques,* as well as many articles and features in other works. Forthcoming publications include books on the SAS, while Chris's wider research interests lie in literature and ancient history. Chris lives in South Wales, U.K.

INDEX

References in italics refer to illustrations